KU-208-699

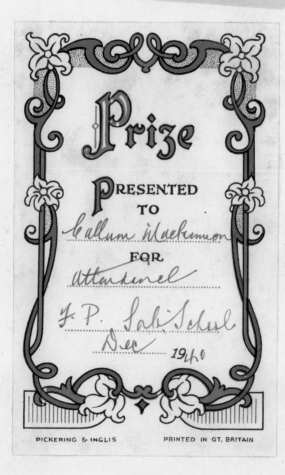

Prize

Presented
to

Callum Mackinnon

for

Attendance

F. P. Sab School

Dec 1940

PICKERING & INGLIS   PRINTED IN GT. BRITAIN

Dwight Lyman Moody

The Prince of Evangelists

BY

WILLIAM ROSS

PICKERING & INGLIS LTD.

LONDON   GLASGOW   MANCHESTER   EDINBURGH

LONDON -   - 14 PATERNOSTER ROW, E.C.4
GLASGOW -   - 229 BOTHWELL STREET, C.3
MANCHESTER - 135 DEANSGATE, 3
EDINBURGH   - 29 GEORGE IV BRIDGE, 1
NEW YORK   - LOIZEAUX BROS., 19 WEST 21st ST.
TORONTO-   - HOME EVANGEL, 418 CHURCH ST., 2

MEMOIR SERIES

OF MIGHTY MEN AND WOMEN

Made and Printed in Great Britain

Contents

Illustrations

DWIGHT LYMAN MOODY

Chapter I

Early Days

D. L. MOODY was born in Northfield, Massachusetts, on 5th February 1837. His father was Edwin Moody, and his mother, Betsy Holton. Both were descended from those brave and hardy " Pilgrim Fathers " who had crossed the Atlantic Ocean two hundred years before in search of freedom of worship. They had a family of seven sons and two daughters. Dwight was the sixth son. Edwin Moody had secured some acres of ground in the neighbourhood. These he occupied his leisure hours in cultivating—a part of his time being given to building work, his profession being a stonemason. He had a hard struggle which he was unable to overcome, and after an illness of a few hours died suddenly when he was forty-one

7

years of age, leaving a large family, to which two additions were made only a month after his death, entirely unprovided for. His widow was earnestly advised to part with her children, keeping only the twin babies, as the burden would be too much for her to bear. She, however, determined to trust in Him who is the Stay of the widow and hath promised to be the Father of the fatherless.

After his father's death Mr. Moody tells us that the creditors came in and swept away everything they had. They took even the kindling wood, and there came on a snowstorm. " Next morning mother said we would have to stay in bed till school-time, because there was no wood to make a fire. Then all at once I heard some one chopping wood, and found it was my Uncle Cyrus. I tell you I have always had a warm heart for that uncle for that act, and that night there came the biggest load of wood I ever saw in my life. It took two yoke of oxen to draw it. It was that uncle that brought it. It has followed me all through life."

The best account of the family at this period is given by Mr. Moody himself. He says : " I can give you a little experience of my own family before I was four years old. The first thing I remember was the death of my father. He had been unfortunate in business, and failed. Soon after his death the creditors came in and took everything. My mother was left with a large family of children. One calamity after another swept over the entire household. Twins were added to the family, and my mother was taken sick. The eldest boy was fifteen years of age, and to him my mother looked as a stay in her calamity. He had been reading some of the trashy novels, and the belief had seized him that he had only to go away to make a fortune. Away he went. I can remember how eagerly she used to look for tidings of that boy; how she used to send us to the post office to see if there was a letter, and I recollect how we used to come back with the sad news, 'No letter.' I remember how in the evenings we used to sit beside her in that New England home and we would talk about our father, but the moment the name of that boy was mentioned, she would hush us into silence. Some nights when the wind was very high, and the house, which was upon a hill, would tremble at every gust, the voice of my mother was raised for that wanderer who had treated her so un-kindly. I used to think she loved him more than all of us put together, and I believe she did. On a Thanksgiving Day—you know that is a family day in New England—she used to set a chair for him, thinking he would return home. When I got so that I could write, I sent letters all over the country, but could find no trace of him. One day while in Boston the news reached me that he had returned. While in that city I remember how I used to look for him in every store—he had a mark on his face—but I never got any trace. One day, while my mother was sitting at the door, a stranger was seen coming toward the house, and when she came to the door he stopped. My mother didn't know her boy. There he stood with folded arms, and great beard flowing down on his breast, and tears trickling down his face. When my mother saw these tears she cried, ' Oh, it is my lost boy,' and entreated him to come in, but he stood there. ' No, mother,' said he, ' I will not come in until I hear that you have forgiven me.' Do you believe she was not willing to forgive him ? Do you think she was likely to keep him standing there ? She rushed to the threshold, threw her arms around him and breathed forgiveness."

A characteristic incident is told of Dwight

when he was six years old. An old rail fence fell upon him, and he found it impossible to escape from it. " Then," said he to himself, " I happened to think that maybe God would help me, and so I asked him, and after that I could lift the rails." Thus he escaped that danger. Very early in life he tells us himself that a deep impression was made upon him by a man who was working with him in the field. He was weeping, and told the lad a story which ever after influenced him. On leaving home, said this man, his mother gave him a text, " Seek first the Kingdom of God," but he paid no heed to it. One Sunday he went into a village church, and the minister gave out his text, " Seek first the Kingdom of God." The text went right to his heart. He thought it was his mother still following him by prayer and entreaty. He went away from that place, and went into another church, and the minister gave out his text, " Seek first the Kingdom of God " ; but in reply his heart said, " No, I will first become rich." He determined to go to church no more ; but after a few months the first place of worship he went into the sermon was preached from the same text. He couldn't get it out of his mind. He was so miserable that he resolved

not to go to God's house ; and he did not go for
several years. His mother died, and he thought
he might become a Christian now, but he felt his
heart hard—hard as the stone in the field which
he moved from the drill with his hoe. Shortly
after this, young Moody went to Boston, where
he was led to give his heart to God, and, curiously
enough, one of his first thoughts was about this
man. He inquired of his own mother regarding
him, only to receive the reply that he had become
insane, and to every one who approached him he
lifted his hands towards the sky and said, " Seek
first the Kingdom of God." On returning home,
Moody at once paid him a visit, and found him
sitting on a rocking-chair. He says, " As soon as
he saw me he pointed at me and said, ' Young
man, seek first the Kingdom of God.' " Such
an incident was fitted to prove a life stimulus to
any earnest man, and was so to the youthful
Dwight.

CHAPTER II

The School of Life

" TRUST in God " was the simple creed which Betsy Moody firmly held and constantly impressed upon her children. An evidence of the thoroughness with which this was taught to little Dwight is seen in an adventure which befell him on one occasion.

It was the late autumn, and Dwight's older brother, a boy of twelve, and himself, aged eight, set out one evening for a farm four miles distant, where they had secured employment during the harvest. When they reached the old ferry across the Connecticut River darkness had fallen. Crossing the fields hand in hand, they hailed the ferryman on the other bank. After some delay, he reached them, and they stepped into his boat only to find the old man in an intoxicated state, and quite unfit to row. As the current swiftly

bore them downstream, they became more and
more alarmed. Then the younger lad took the
hand of his brother, and, repeating the oft-
expressed phrase of their mother, began to cheer
him. God, said he, would watch over them and
protect them even in their present danger. The
hope so trustfully uttered did not go unanswered,
and in due course they landed safely at the other
side.

Mrs. Moody was a tender-hearted woman,
from whose door the hungry were never turned
away. She early taught Dwight and his brothers
and sisters the privilege and happiness of helping
others. Once, when they were about to sit down
to an all-too-scanty supper, a poor beggar came
to the door. The need of the man being made
known to the children, they at once offered to
have their own slices cut thinner, so that he
might have share.

Among other things, this Puritan mother taught
that a promise given must be kept at all costs.
Dwight, on one occasion, went to work for a
neighbour during the winter months in return
for his keep. Complaining that he had had to
eat corn-meal and milk for nineteen consecutive
meals, the boy wished to be released from his

agreement. His mother, however, ruled that while there was not much variety there was at least abundance, and sent him back to his work.

Yet, though kindly, Dwight's mother was very strict, and the boy, a leader in pranks and mischief, frequently came in for measures of discipline. These, in true boy fashion, he would try to dodge, as he afterwards loved to tell. " Mother would send me out for a stick, and I thought I could fool her and get a dead one. But she would snap the stick and then tell me to get another. She was rarely in a hurry, and certainly never when she was whipping me. Once I told her that the whipping did not hurt at all. I never had occasion to tell her so again, for she put it on so that it did hurt."

His devotion to his mother was very remarkable all through life. Even after he became absorbed in evangelistic work he never forgot to write his mother frequently, and to give her an account of all that was going on. She received the great blessing of her life at a service in North- field, conducted by her son, in 1875. She was a woman of very strong mind but of stronger heart, and by her power of affection she controlled all her family and bound them to her by a tie

that could not be broken. Amongst them all,
none was more devoted and loyal than Dwight.
When, at the age of ninety-one, she passed away
in January 1896, he paid this great tribute to her :
" She made home so pleasant ! I thought so
much of my mother, and cannot say half enough.
That dear face—there was no sweeter face on
earth ! Fifty years I have been coming back,
and was always glad to get back. When I got
within fifty miles of home, I always grew restless,
and walked up and down the car. It seemed to
me as if the train would never get to Northfield.
For sixty-eight years she lived on that hill, and
when I came back after dark I always looked to
see the light in mother's window. It was because
she made our home so happy that she started me
thinking how to make happy homes for others."
To this brave and earnest mother the world owes
a great debt of gratitude, for it was largely her
influence which moulded the character of her
famous son.

Yet Mr. Moody never forgot the poverty and
hardships of his boyhood's days ; and the
memory of them helped to make him the sympathetic man he became. " I had been in the
world only three or four years," said he on one

occasion, " when my father died a bankrupt, and
the creditors came and swept away almost everything we had. My widow mother had a cow and
a few things, but it was a hard struggle to keep
the wolf from the door. My brother went to
Greenfield, and secured work in a store for his
board, and went to school. It was so lonely there
that he wanted me to get a place so as to be near
him. But I didn't want to leave home. One
cold day in November my brother came home
and said he had a place for me. I said that I
wouldn't go ; but after it was talked over they
decided I should go. I didn't want my brothers
to know that I hadn't the courage to go ; but that
night was a long one.

" The next morning we started. We went up
on the hill and had a last sight of the old house.
We sat down there and cried. I thought that
would be the last time I should ever see that old
home. I cried all the way down to Greenfield.
There my brother introduced me to a man who
was so old he couldn't milk his cows and do the
chores ; so I was to do his errands, milk the
cows, and go to school. I looked at the old man
and saw he was cross. I took a good look at the
wife, and thought she was crosser than the old

man. I stayed there an hour, and it seemed like a week. I went round then to my brother, and said :

" ' I am going home.'

" ' What are you going home for ? '

" ' I am homesick,' I said.

" ' Oh, well, you will get over it in a few days.'

" ' I never will,' I said. ' I don't want to.'

" He said : ' You will get lost if you start for home now ; it is getting dark.'

" I was frightened then, as I was only about ten years old, and I said : ' I will go at daybreak to-morrow morning.'

" He took me to a shop-window where they had some jack-knives and other things, and tried to divert my mind. What did I care for those old jack-knives ? I wanted to get back home to my mother and brothers. It seemed as if my heart was breaking.

" All at once my brother said : ' Dwight, there comes a man who will give you a cent.'

" ' How do you know he will ? ' I asked.

" ' Oh ! he gives every new boy that comes to town a cent.'

" I brushed away the tears, for I wouldn't have him see me crying, and I got right in the middle of the side-walk, where he couldn't help but see me, and kept my eyes right upon him. I remember how that old man looked as he came tottering down the side-walk. Oh, such a bright, cheerful, sunny face he had! When he came opposite to where I was, he stopped, took my hat off, put his hand on my head, and said to my brother :

" ' This is a new boy in town, isn't it ? '

" ' Yes, sir, he is ; just came to-day.'

" I watched to see if he would put his hand into his pocket. I was thinking of that cent. He began to talk to me so kindly that I forgot all about it. He told me that God had an only Son, and He sent Him down here, and wicked men killed Him ; and he said He died for me. He only talked five minutes, but he took me captive. After he had given me this little talk, he put his hand in his pocket and took out a brand-new cent—a copper that looked just like gold. He gave me that ; I thought it was gold—and didn't I hold it tight ! I never felt so rich before or since. I don't know what became of that cent. I have always regretted that I didn't keep it ; but I can feel the pressure of the old man's hand on my head to-day. Fifty years have rolled away, and I can hear those kind words ringing yet. I never shall forget that act. He put the money at usury : that cent has cost me a great many dollars. I have never walked up the streets of this country, or the old country, but down into my pocket goes my hand, and I take out some money and give it to every forlorn, miserable child I see. I think how the old man lifted a load from me, and I want to lift a load from some one else."

Chapter III

Leaving Home

YOUNG Moody obtained a very scanty education at the local village school, which he was only able to attend on odd days, having to earn money as work offered itself on surrounding farms. When at school he was a leader in mischief, and frequently deserved and received the usual strokes with the "rattan cane." There came to that school, however, a new teacher who favoured other methods. She intimated to the astonished boys that she proposed to dispense with the old-time whippings.

Looking back upon those scenes long after, Moody described what transpired in these words : " I happened to be at the school at that time, and we said to each other that we were going to have a grand time that winter. There would be no more corporal punishment, and we were going to be ruled by love. The new teacher was a lady, and she opened the school with prayer. We hadn't seen it done before, and we were impressed, especially when she prayed that she might have grace and strength to rule the school with love. The school went on for several weeks, and we saw no cane. I was one of the first to break the rules of the school. The teacher asked me to stay behind. I thought the cane was coming out again, and I was in a fighting mood. She took me alone. She sat down and began to talk to me kindly. That was worse than the cane. I did not like it. She said : ' I have made up my mind that if I cannot control the school by love, I will give it up. I will have no punishment. If you love me, try to keep the rules of the school.' "

This was too much for young Moody, who felt a lump rising in his throat. " You will never have any more trouble with me," he replied, " and I will whack the first boy that gives you any trouble ! " And the next day, to the great surprise of his chums and to the equally great consternation of his teacher, he carried his threat into action.

The extent of his education may be judged by the account given of him not long afterwards by his uncle. Said he : " When Dwight reads his

Bible out loud he couldn't make anything more out of it than he could out of the chattering of a lot of blackbirds. Many of the words were so far beyond the boy that he left them out entirely, and the majority of the others he mangled fearfully."

Where frolic and practical joking were concerned, however, he was always in the forefront. The village Squire, whose residence adjoined the little red schoolhouse, was a handy victim. Once, it is told, young Dwight led an attack against the Squire's cattle-sheds. Quietly the boys climbed up on to the rafters, then suddenly set up a chorus of blood-curdling whoops and yells, dancing about on the loose planks as they did so. The young steers below were soon in a panic of fear and rushed excitedly through the barn-yard fences. By the time the alarmed Squire reached the scene, the boys were off the roof, and, led by Dwight, were, with innocent diligence, helping to round up the stampeding cattle.

During one rather uneventful winter, he decided that something must be done to rouse the interest of the villagers. Without confiding in even his closest companion, he wrote out, and posted on the schoolhouse door, a notice announcing a temperance meeting to be addressed on a certain date by a lecturer from a nearby town. The night arrived, and with it the audience at the little schoolroom, which had been duly warmed and lighted for the occasion. But no lecturer put in an appearance !

Although those early days were days of want and hardship, how full of fun they were ! On one occasion, at the break-up of the school session, the villagers were invited to a school display. It fell to young Moody to recite Mark Antony's classic speech over the dead body of Julius Cæsar. To add to the dramatic effect, the reciter had a small box, to serve as the coffin, set up on the teacher's desk. Dwight was in the midst of an eloquent oration, in which he indulged in the most extravagant gestures. With one of these he knocked the lid from off the box, and out jumped a badly scared old cat, while a hilarious audience rocked with laughter.

A few years later, bidding good-bye to his schooldays, he went to work in a printer's business in Clinton. His task was to write the addresses on the wrappers of a local paper. The country youth, with no experience of crowded streets and numbered tenements, soon became hopelessly muddled, and was discharged. Returning home, he resumed doing odd work on the farms around Northfield.

One day in the early spring of 1854, while cutting logs with his brother Edwin on the hillside, he exclaimed abruptly : " I'm tired of this ! I'm not going to stay around here any longer. I'm going to the city." Despite all attempts to dissuade him, he set out to make his way to Boston, a hundred miles away. On the way he met another brother, George, who, on hearing his determined purpose, gave him five dollars, which just paid his fare.

In due course he reached Boston, without money, but with plenty of grit and eagerness. In that city he had two uncles in the boot and shoe trade, Samuel and Lemuel Holton. With his Uncle Lemuel he found board and lodging, while he tramped around Boston in search of work. Like many another youth similarly placed, he found this no easy task. Long afterwards, preaching in that same city, he described those trying days. " I remember," said he, " how I walked up and down the streets trying to find a situation, and I recollect how, when they answered me roughly, their treatment would chill my soul. . . . It seemed as if there was room for every one else in the world, but none for me. For about two days I had the feeling that nobody wanted me. I never have had it since, and I never want it again. It is an awful feeling. It seems to me that must have been the feeling of the Son of God when He was down here. They did not want Him. He had come to save men, and they did not want to be saved. He had come to lift men up, and they did not want to be lifted up.

" I went to the post office two or three times a day to see if there was a letter for me. I knew there was not as there was but one mail a day from Northfield. I had no employment and was very homesick, and so I went constantly to the post office, thinking perhaps that when the mail had come in my letter had been mislaid. At last, however, I got a letter. It was from my youngest sister—the first letter she ever wrote me. I opened it with a light heart, thinking there was some good news from home, but the burden of the whole letter was that she had heard there were pickpockets in Boston and warned me to beware of them. I thought that I had better get some money in hand first, and then I might look out for pickpockets ! "

By the end of the week he was utterly discouraged and ready to humbly accept the advice of his Uncle Lemuel. Acting upon it, he approached his Uncle Samuel, and was soon settled in his boot store. " Dwight, I am afraid if you come in here you will want to run the store yourself," said Uncle Samuel Holton at that interview. " Now, my men here want to do their work as I want it done. If you want to come in here and do the best you can and do it right, and if you'll be willing to ask whenever you don't know, and if you promise to go to church and Sunday school, and if you will not go anywhere that you wouldn't want your mother to know about, we'll see how we can get along. You can have till Monday to think it over."

" I don't want till Monday," was the prompt reply of the lad. " I'll promise now." Thus he entered upon his first post in the city of Boston. From the beginning he displayed the marks of a successful business man, in perseverance, tact, and originality. These characteristics, too, he carried into the greater business of his later life, the splendid work of bringing men and women into the kingdom of Jesus Christ.

Chapter IV

Conversion and Early Service

SHORTLY after settling in Boston, he attended the meetings of Dr. E. M. Kirk, at Mount Vernon Congregational Church. He joined the Sunday - school class taught by Edward D. Kimbal, a devoted and earnest Christian. Mr. Moody himself tells his experience at that time. "When I was in Boston I used to attend a Sunday-school class, and one day I recollect my teacher came around behind the counter of the shop where I was at work, put his hand upon my shoulder, and talked to me about Christ and my soul. I hadn't found that I had a soul till then. I said to myself, 'This is a very strange thing. Here is a man who never saw me till lately, and he is weeping over my sins, and I never wept over them myself.' But I understand it now, and know what it is to pray for men's souls and weep over their sins."

Of this vital and far-reaching transaction, Mr. Kimbal gives an account in these words : " I determined to speak to him about Christ and about his soul, and started down to Holton's shoe store. When I was nearly there I began to wonder whether I ought to go in just then during business hours. I thought that possibly my call might embarrass the boy, and that when I went away the other clerks would ask who I was, and taunt him with my efforts in trying to make him a good boy. In the meantime I had passed the store, and, discovering this, I determined to make a dash for it and have it over at once. I found Moody in the back part of the building wrapping up shoes. I went up to him at once, and putting my hand on his shoulder, I made what I afterwards felt was a very weak plea for Christ. I don't know just what words I used, nor could Mr. Moody tell. I simply told him of Christ's love for him and the love Christ wanted in return. That was all there was. It seemed the young man was just ready for the light that then broke upon him, and there, in the back of that store in Boston, he gave himself and his life to Christ." This was the deciding point in his life. Shortly thereafter he applied for admission to the Church, and after some time of trial was admitted.

He at once sought to witness for Christ, although in a very awkward way, in the Y.M.C.A. meetings and elsewhere in connection with the Church. Still he persevered, and eventually became clear and definite in regard to the great lines of Christian truth, the Bible being his text-book, his manual of theology, and his Christian workers' guide. He left Boston for Chicago in 1856, longing for a field of Christian labour, and impatient to be at the work of winning souls. He obtained a situation in the shoe shop of Mr. Wiswall. Although rough, uncouth, and somewhat boisterous in manner, he soon became the best salesman in the employment of the firm, and succeeded in a remarkable way with such customers as were unusually difficult to handle. An extension to the business gave him a larger opportunity of displaying his peculiar talent. In discussing the questions of the day, he naturally felt that he was limited on every side by the defects of his early educa-tion ; still, there was a native force within him, which urged him forward, and he usually succeeded in stating clearly and conclusively the particular view which he upheld. He joined the Plymouth Congregational Church, the minister of which was Dr. J. E. Roy. It was a working, kindly, practical church. He at once took five pews, and kept them filled with young men at every service. In the streets he found boys and girls to form his Sunday-school class. His success in this particular work was very remarkable. The very first Lord's Day after he got liberty to teach a class, he appeared with eighteen young people, dirty, unkempt, some of them barefoot, but every one with a soul to save; and these formed his first class. This proved to be an opening into a very large work, for in visiting these children he was led into some of the worst districts of the city, where public-houses abound, and sailors' boarding-houses are constantly met with. A large lapsed population also he met with in the neighbourhood of the docks. Here he met with a fellow-worker, Mr. J. B. Stillson, who gave all his spare time to this work. The two at once determined to unite their energies, and it is said in a single summer they recruited no less than twenty mission Sunday schools. Mr. Moody was not satisfied that he had reached the lowest stratum, nor that any other agency had as yet done so. On the north side of the city there was a district named the " Sands," sometimes also called " Little Hell." Here crime and vice reigned, and here he began to work on his own account. A crazy building that formerly had been a public-house, he secured, and determined to fill it with the young people from the street, and in a short time he had his place overflowing. So far Mr. Moody was not particularly good at the executive part of his work, but made up for his lack by an untiring store of zeal and energy.

He resolved that every day he would speak to at least one person about Christ. One evening, it is related, he had retired to rest when it suddenly flashed across his mind that he had not spoken to any one on that theme during the whole day. Quitting his bed, he rose and went down to the street. It was raining heavily, and he felt inclined to re-enter the house. Then he saw a stranger approaching, holding an umbrella above him. Moody politely begged for shelter, and the man readily granted it. Off they walked under the one umbrella, Moody preaching the Gospel and pressing the claims of Christ the

MR. MOODY WITH SOME OF HIS 1500 BIBLE CLASS MEMBERS

The pupils of this class were guttersnipes drawn from the lowest and the most neglected elements of Chicago society

D. L. MOODY AND HIS
GUTTERSNIPES

Members of his Bible Class, who loved him
so much that they formed an escort for him

while. Before that walk was ended, another
soul had been won to the Saviour.

One night a friend called upon him during
those early Chicago days and found him teach-
ing a poor negro boy. Said he to the visitor
by way of explanation : " I have got only one
talent. I have no education, but I love the
Lord Jesus Christ, and I want to do something
for Him. I wish you to pray for me."

The open-air meetings held in connection
with his work enabled him to reach more than
a hundred public-houses and to extend the
influence of his mission. The school was entirely
unfurnished, even with seats, and the material
to be worked on was of the very roughest kind.
In a short time the building became too small
for the work, and the school was removed to a
large hall over the North Market. As it was
without furniture, Mr. Moody applied to several
friends to help them. This brought him into
contact with Mr. Farwell, who, in a short time,
was nominated by Mr. Moody superintendent
of the school. The duties attaching to this
position he discharged nobly for more than
six years. Of the hall and the duties of its leader,
the following description has been given : " It

was a large, dingy, dilapidated-looking brick
building on the outside, while the inside was
a great grimy hall with blackened walls and
ceiling, and as bare and uninviting as can be
imagined. But it was soon crowded to the
doors with classes of boys and girls of a type
entirely new to me ; largely the gamins of the
streets, bold, restless, inquisitive youngsters,
whose wardrobe was often limited to trousers,
shirt, and suspenders—even these in a very
advanced stage of decay. The scholars were
bubbling over with mischief and exuberance
of vitality and sorely tried the patience of the
teachers ; but the singing was a vent for their
spirits, and such singing I had never heard
before. The boys who sold papers in the street
had an indescribable lung power, and the rest
seemed not far behind. There must have been
five or six hundred scholars, and it was no easy
task to govern such a boisterous crowd, but the
teachers seemed to interest their classes, and
the exercises passed off with great enthusiasm.

" At the close of the school Mr. Moody took
his place at the door and seemed to know personally every boy and girl ; he shook hands and
had a smile and a cheery word for each. They

crowded about him tumultuously, and his arm must have ached many a time after those meetings. It was easy to see the hold he had on those young lives, and why they were drawn to that place week after week. The institution was a veritable hive of activity—meetings almost every evening, with occasional picnics and socials, and services on the Sabbath that occupied most of the day."

It was very difficult work to get teachers who could interest and command such pupils as were got to attend. In a short time it was found desirable to let the class choose which teacher to attend, and thus the dull teachers disappeared from having nothing to do, and the men of mark, the survivals of the fittest, were allowed to remain. In three months there were 200 attending, in six months 350, and within a year the average attendance was 650, and occasionally as many as a thousand would be present. A surprise visit by President Lincoln, at Mr. Farwell's request, proved an event in the history of the school never to be forgotten, and when six months afterwards the President asked for 75,000 volunteers, no fewer than 60 boys, who had heard him, answered the call.

How full of activity these Sundays in the old North Market Hall were may be gathered from these recollections of the evangelist himself :

" I didn't know much at this time. But after going from early morning until late at night, with only a few crackers and cheese, I was faint and fatigued. Sometimes, after such a day I imagined that I sinned in going to sleep over my prayers when, actually, I was a fool for neglecting the dictates of common sense. God is not a hard taskmaster ; and, in later years, I have learned, that to do your best work, you cannot afford to neglect the common laws of health."

Mr. Moody's work among the poor and wretched made him a thoroughgoing total abstainer. He was the more convinced of the necessity of being out and out on the temperance question the longer and the harder he worked. He came to see quite clearly that the mightiest obstacle to the progress and power of the Gospel was strong drink.

In a short time he began to be asked to attend conferences and conventions. In going to one of these, along with the secretary of a Christian association, he arrived at two o'clock in the morning. Sleep was out of the question. They resolved to spend the time in prayer. As the hour of meeting was approaching, Mr. Moody secured a room quite near the hall where the convention was to be held. When asked what he wanted to do with this room, he said, " I want it for an inquiry room." Both of the young men felt that God was going to give them souls, and each agreed that while the other spoke he would pray for him. Mr. Moody's speaking on that day was very striking. He told the Sunday-school teachers of their absolute helplessness without Christ, characterised the terrible sin of doing the work of the Lord de-ceitfully, and after an hour's earnest speaking, asked all the teachers who wished to have power in their life-work to accompany him into the schoolroom next door. A large number did so, and were helped to realise their life-ministry in the salvation of the young. A widespread revival resulted from this effort, which proved to be a new revelation to Mr. Moody himself. Several leading men who at that time took up evangelistic work met in different parts of the country. They became deeply convinced that they needed more of the power of the Holy Ghost. They believed that the risen Christ had this gift for them, and they were determined to obtain it.

The Springfield Annual Convention was at hand, and Mr. Moody, Mr. Jacobs, and Major Whittle arrived before the Convention began. They set about holding meetings at once, and no fewer than seventy persons were brought into the Kingdom. The following year the Sunday-school workers met in the city of Decatur, where intelligence was brought that no fewer than 10,000 had been brought to Christ in one year. From that time Mr. Moody was in constant request all over the United States, and he brought into his work a purpose, an earnestness, and, by God's blessing, a success that was very remarkable.

CHAPTER V

Soul-Winning and Organising

MR. MOODY was a born commander and organiser, and whatever came in the way of the success of his work must move out of the way, or suffer the severest attack. In this way we account for his zeal in the temperance cause, and his so prevailing upon a family who had a quantity of whisky wherewith to begin a carousal, that when he asked leave to give them a few words of an address, so earnest and so convincing was he that they permitted him to pour the drink into the gutter.

He soon became a favourite speaker at conventions and conferences. He gave himself right loyally to the work of the Christian Association in Chicago. The noon meeting was reorganised and very largely attended. He successfully brought the mission schools into connection with the churches in the districts where they were located. The result of his evangelistic work gave him special concern. He endeavoured to get those who had been brought under impression into connection with the churches in their neighbourhood ; but in this he was not successful. With the readiness of mind which he possessed, he saw quite clearly, and others have since learned, that unless they were organised into a church they would be certain to drift, and so the idea came to him of starting what eventually became the Chicago Avenue Congregation. The labourer is worthy of his hire, and the congregation that does the work will reap the harvest. His ideal was to have a congregation at work ; every member to have something to do ; every night a service. The result of all this was practically what has been experienced elsewhere, a continuous revival.

He was elected President of the Young Men's Christian Association, and succeeded in raising money for new buildings. Farwell Hall, as the main building was called, became a great religious centre, and it may be truly said that thousands were led to Christ within its walls.

It was at this period he was joined in the work by Ira D. Sankey, who tells in the following words how the union came to be formed :

" In 1870, with two or three others, I was appointed a delegate to the International Convention of the Association, to be held at Indianapolis that year. It was announced that Mr. Moody would lead a morning prayer-meeting at 7 o'clock. I was rather late, and therefore sat down near the door with a Presbyterian minister, Mr. Robert McMillan, a delegate from my own county, who said to me, ' Mr. Sankey, the singing here has been abominable ; I wish you would start up something when that man stops praying, if he ever does.' I promised him to do so ; and when opportunity offered I sang the familiar hymn, ' There is a fountain filled with blood.' The congregation joined heartily, and a brighter aspect seemed to be given to the meeting.

"At the conclusion of the meeting Mr. McMillan said to me : ' Let me introduce you to Mr. Moody.' We joined the little procession of persons who were going up to shake hands with him ; and thus I met for the first time the man with whom, in the providence of God, I was to be associated for the remainder of his life, nearly thirty years.

" Moody's first words to me, after my introduction, were, ' Where are you from ? Are you married ?　What is your business ? '　Upon telling him that I lived in Pennsylvania, was married, had two children, and was in Government employ, he said in his characteristic manner, ' You will have to give that up.'

"I stood amazed, at a loss to understand why the man should tell me that I would have to give up what I considered a good position. ' What for ? ' I exclaimed.

"' To come to Chicago and help me in my work,' was the answer.

"When I told him that I could not leave my business, he retorted, ' You must ; I have been looking for you for the last eight years.' "

In six months Mr. Sankey was out of business, and, alongside of Mr. Moody, was working hard to win souls. Mr. Sankey soon began to feel his conscious need of spiritual power. During Mr. Moody's absence in London, attending the Mild-may Conference, the responsibility of the work at home devolved upon Mr. Sankey. It was then that he received a special filling of the Holy Ghost. The blessing upon his singing after this was multiplied an hundredfold.

Along with many other buildings, Farwell Hall suffered in the disastrous fire of 1871 ; but the last service held in it made upon Mr. Moody a lasting impression and changed the manner of his working in all his after life. The subject that evening was, " What shall I do with Jesus ? " We have heard him tell the story with thrilling interest to a body of Christian workers. He had just been about the close of his address when the fire-bell rang ; but that sound was very familiar in Chicago. The last sentence of his address was, " Now, I want you to take the question with you and think over it till we meet next week." He afterwards said, " What a mistake ! It seemed as if Satan was in my mind when I said this. Since then I have never dared to give an audience a week to think on their salvation. If they were lost they might rise up in judgment against me. ' Now is the accepted time.' " This was the key-note of all his speaking for the remainder of life.

Here is Mr. Sankey's description of the appalling conflagration :

" On my return to Chicago I learned that Mr. Moody, after reaching his home on the North Side, had aroused his sleeping neighbours, assisted men and women into conveyances, and urged them to flee for their lives. As the billows of fire came nearer and nearer, Mr. Moody, with his wife and children, made his way into the north-western district to a place of safety beyond the fire line. Before leaving her home Mrs. Moody took down from the wall an oil painting of her husband and asked him to carry it with him; but he declined, saying that he did not think it would look well for him to be running through the streets of Chicago with his picture in his arms at such a time! Speaking of the fire to a friend some time later, Mr. Moody remarked:

" ' All I saved was my Bible, my family, and my reputation.'

" Mr. Moody and I continued to hold services and to help the poor and needy who had lost everything in the fire. We slept together in a corner of the new Tabernacle, with nothing for a bed but a single lounge; and frequently the fierce prairie winds would blow the drifting snow into our room."

It may well be imagined that a man of Mr. Moody's temperament—strong, active, unsparing of self, and yet at the same time having business claims upon him of a very definite kind—must frequently be in a strait betwixt business and Christian work. He devoted himself to his business as formerly, doing it very heartily, but

every evening and every Sunday was wholly
given up to Christ. Having changed his situation, the new firm found it to their advantage to
make him do the work of a commercial traveller.
This interfered very seriously with his evening
work; but he always contrived to get home for
the Lord's Day, that he might be at his Sunday
school and other work. The question forced
itself upon him, in a short time, whether his
business or his mission work must have his
entire devotion, and at once, after deep thought
and prayer, he decided to give up all his business
connection, and give himself wholly and un-
reservedly to practical work for the Master.

At one time he thought it was within his power
to become wealthy, great, and powerful, and that
thus he might become the liberal benefactor of
the cause of Christ. Now he saw that by throwing
himself personally into the work he could do far
more for it and in it than by any amount of wealth
bestowed upon it; but where was the means for
doing this work to come from? He said to Mr.
Jacobs, an intimate friend, " I have decided to
give God all my time." " But how are you going
to live? " he was asked. To this he answered,
" God will provide for me if He wishes me to

keep on, and I shall keep on until I am obliged
to stop."

He left his employers in the kindliest possible
spirit, and they felt convinced that the man who
served them well and faithfully would undoubtedly
be successful in that to which he had given his
whole heart ; but the new work was not strange
to him.   It was simply the harvest of what he
had been sowing since 1865.   He set aside a
large part of his earnings while in business to
maintain him till the work would be strong, but
in a short time it was seen that the amount did
not more than meet half the demands which were
made upon him.

He had been reading the life of George Muller,
of Bristol.   It made a great impression upon him,
and he was led to believe for himself that it was
better to trust in God than to trust in princes.

He was at times reduced to great straits.   Some
friends wondered how he was enabled to live.
They believed, however, it was their duty to
help him.   They did so, and those who knew
the man and his labour for the Lord esteemed it
the highest privilege to supply his needs.

Perhaps the best account of the entire situation
is to be found in his own words : " I never lost

sight of Jesus Christ since the first night I met Him in the store in Boston. But for years I was only a nominal Christian, really believing that I could not work for God. No one had ever asked me to do anything.

" I went to Chicago, I hired five pews in a church, and used to go out to the street and pick up young men to fill these pews. I never spoke to these young men about their souls ; that was the work of the elders, I thought. After working for some time like that, I started a mission Sunday school. I thought numbers were everything, and so I worked for numbers. When the attendance ran below one thousand it troubled me ; and when it ran to twelve or fifteen hundred I was elated. Still none were converted ; there was no harvest. Then God opened my eyes.

" There was a class of young ladies in the school, who were, without exception, the most frivolous set of girls I ever met. One Sunday the teacher was ill, and I took that class. They laughed in my face, and I felt like opening the door and telling them all to get out and never come back. That week the teacher of the class came into the place where I worked. He was pale and looked very ill. ' What is the trouble ? '

I asked. 'I have had another hæmorrhage of my lungs. The doctor says I cannot live on Lake Michigan, so I am going to New York State. I suppose I am going home to die.'

"He seemed greatly troubled, and when I asked him the reason, he replied, 'Well, I have never led any of my class to Christ. I really believe I have done the girls more harm than good.' I had never heard any one talk like that before, and it set me thinking. After a while I said, 'Suppose you go and tell them how you feel. I will go with you in a carriage if you wish to go.'

"He consented, and we started out together. It was one of the best journeys I ever had on earth. We went to the house of one of the girls, called for her, and the teacher talked to her of her soul. There was no laughing then. Tears stood in her eyes before long. After he had explained the way of life he suggested that we have prayer. He asked me to pray. True, I had never done such a thing in my life as to pray to God to convert a young lady there and then, but we prayed, and God answered our prayer. We went to other houses. He would go upstairs, and be all out of breath, and he would tell

D. L. MOODY PREACHING TO A CROWDED AUDIENCE IN ONE OF THE VAST LONDON HALLS

MR. MOODY PREACHING, ON EASTER AFTERNOON, AT "THE HILL CALLED CALVARY," OUTSIDE JERUSALEM, TO A LARGE AUDIENCE COMPOSED OF JEWS, MOHAMMEDANS, AND NOMINAL CHRISTIANS

the girls what he had come for. It wasn't long before they broke down, and sought salvation.

" When his strength gave out I took him back to his lodgings. The next day we went out again. At the end of ten days he came to the store with his face literally shining. ' Mr. Moody,' he said, ' the last one of my class has yielded herself to Christ.' I tell you we had a time of rejoicing. He had to leave the next night, so I called his class together that night for a prayer-meeting, and there God kindled a fire in my soul that has never gone out. The height of my ambition had been to be a successful merchant, and if I had known that meeting was going to take that ambition out of me I might not have gone. But how many times I have thanked God since for that meeting. The dying teacher sat in the midst of his class, and talked with them, and read the fourteenth chapter of John. We tried to sing, ' Blest be the tie that binds,' after which we knelt down in prayer. I was just rising from my knees when one of the class began to pray for her dying teacher. Another prayed, and another, and before we rose the whole class had prayed. As I went out I said to

4

myself, ' O God, let me die rather than lose the blessing I have received to-night.'

" The next morning I went to the depot to say good-bye to that teacher. Just before the train started, one of the class came, and before long, without any prearrangement, they were all there. What a meeting that was. We tried to sing, but we broke down. The last we saw of that dying teacher he was standing on the platform of the car, his finger pointing upward, telling that class to meet him in heaven. I didn't know what this was going to cost me. I was disqualified for business ; it had become distasteful for me. I had got a taste of another world, and cared no more for making money. For some days after the greatest struggle of my life took place. Should I give up business and give myself to Christian work, or should I not ? I have never regretted my choice. Oh, the luxury of leading some one out of the darkness of this world into the glorious light and liberty of the Gospel ! "

On the 28th of August 1862 he took one of the most important steps in his life when he married Miss Emma C. Revell, a young lady who had given herself heartily and loyally to the work. They started their home life in a small cottage.

As might be supposed, from Mr. Moody's peculiar ideas about salary, they were oftentimes in straits but never in real distress. Mr. Sankey's testimony here is very valuable. He says, " I want to say that one of the greatest influences of his life came from his wife. She has been the brake upon an impetuous nature, and she, more than any other person, is responsible for his success."

There were three children born to them— William Revell Moody, his eldest son, who has written the large biography of his father, a work which has met, as might have been expected, with a very large circulation. He is married to the eldest daughter of Major Whittle. Emma, his second child, is the wife of Mr. A. P. Fitt, who for many years was a valued helper in the work ; and Paul, the youngest child, was a student at Yale College, and New College, Edinburgh, where he made his influence felt for good.

It may be convenient, for the purposes of this narrative, to review the remainder of Mr. Moody's life in three distinct lines. First, his work in Great Britain and Ireland ; secondly, his work in America as an evangelist ; and third, his efforts to train Christian workers for service.

CHAPTER VI

First British Campaign

IT was on 7th June 1873 that Mr. Moody and Mr. Sankey, and their families, left for Great Britain, and shortly thereafter began what proved to be their first great missionary campaign. Their work was begun in England. Mr. Moody had asked the Lord to make him the means of winning ten thousand souls for Christ. Strange to say, the two friends who had invited him to this country—Mr. Pennefather and Mr. Cuthbert Bainbridge—had both of them died recently, and Mr. Moody felt for the moment quite disappointed; but he seemed to be more thrown upon God than formerly. He arrived in York, as one of the biographers says, " unheralded and unknown." Only eight persons attended the first meeting. The Sunday served to increase the number, but it was only in the second week that a very distinct and marked improvement took place, and from the very beginning large congregations attended. After a month's labours many professed conversion ; but the results were not by any means what Mr. Moody had looked for. They then went to Newcastle, and here the blessing descended almost as soon as the work began, and five of the principal churches were simultaneously offered for the services to be held. Before the end of a fortnight the largest of the buildings failed to contain the audiences. The blessing spread to all the neighbouring towns and villages. It was felt to be of the first importance that the name and residence of the inquirers should be kept, in order that afterwards they might be led into proper church connection. It was manifest now that a great Revival was in progress. At the end of the month's labours it was found that hundreds of Christian workers were greatly stimulated, and that many of the converts had already been received into the churches. From Newcastle they removed to Scotland, and started their Scottish campaign in Edinburgh, in the Free Assembly Hall, a building capable of holding two thousand with comfort. God was pleased to pour out His Spirit in a very remarkable way.

There were large numbers of inquirers at every service, and it is not too much to say that thousands were led to decide for Christ.

The watch-night service, which completed the work of the year 1873, was probably the most remarkable ever held in the capital of Scotland. It lasted for full five hours, and even then the audience was far from being exhausted. It was followed by a remarkable conference on the 4th of January. It is said that upwards of three thousand people were received into the Church as the fruit of this great work. After a short visit to Dundee, the campaign began in Glasgow on the 8th of February, when Mr. Moody met three thousand Sunday-school teachers, and others. At evening time the City Hall was filled, and four churches in the neighbourhood were filled with the overflow. From the first it was manifest that many who were in the habit of regularly attending church, and a large proportion of whom were members in full communion, had nevertheless but a nominal spiritual life. To these the blessing first came. It extended, however, until the great masses of the people who were without God and without hope were brought into sympathy with the movement and yielded to the power of the Gospel. This continued all the time until 16th April, when a great conference of Christian workers met in the Kibble Palace, Kelvinside. It was estimated that between five and six thousand people were present on that memorable day. On the following Sunday the building was full to overflowing, but there were more people outside than inside. Mr. Moody, with that quick perception that characterised him, at once saw the great importance of speaking from the carriage right in the heart of the vast throng that surrounded him. Those inside immediately joined the crowd outside. When he had finished preaching, inquirers were asked to go inside, and the great hall was filled with a vast audience intensely in earnest about spiritual things, and before the day closed great numbers had yielded themselves to Christ. A short visit to Edinburgh preceded their march northwards. Perth, Montrose, Aberdeen, Inverness, and other places were visited. As it was drawing towards summertime, great meetings were held in the open air. At Aberdeen upwards of twelve thousand attended the open-air services, and right to the very north of Scotland great blessing attended the evangelists.

His first visit to Scotland finished up with a run to Kintyre, beginning with Campbeltown, where he made one of the most valued friendships of his life—that of Mr. and Mrs. Peter M'Kinnon. He proceeded northwards by Killean, Clachan, and Tarbert. From thence he came to Rothesay. Arrangements had been made for his speaking in two churches as he had resolved not to speak in the open air, his work here being simply a passing service. He declined, however, to speak in two places, and the West Free Church, that of Dr. Elder, being the largest, was chosen. Before he was five minutes in the church he felt that a mistake had been made, and he said to Mr. Ross, of Chapelhill, " I begin to feel sea-sick already. What is to be done? " Mr. Ross replied, " The open air is the only place now left." He said, " Can you get me a table to stand on? " " Oh yes, and ample accommodation." The table was provided with a chair on it. The audience gathered — between two and three thousand people—in the open air, just in the dusk. While Mr. Moody preached the lightnings played upon the Cowal Hills. A large number attended the inquiry meeting after the service, and some of the finest workers for Christ at home and abroad came out of that night's work.

The British Association of that year held their annual gathering in Belfast. The opening address by Professor Tyndall, " On Matter," was memorable, and roused the hostility of all believing people. On the second day after delivery part of it was corrected by W. Robertson Smith, of Aberdeen, and on the Sunday evening the largest church in Belfast was crowded, when Professor Watts, in his own inimitable way, replied to the attacks made upon the Christian faith. Several of the earnest and leading men of the city were deeply concerned as to what the effects of Professor Tyndall's address might be in strengthening infidelity or creating indifference to religion. Dr. William Johnstone, who was then a real power in Belfast on the side of religion, said to the writer of these lines, " What is the best thing to be done ? " The answer was given, " God has His own way of answering such attacks. A revival of religion is usually the Divine method of meeting the foe. ' When the enemy cometh in like a flood the Spirit of the

Lord lifteth up a standard against him.' You
had better send an invitation to Mr. Moody
and Mr. Sankey to visit Belfast, and if God gives
you such a blessing as He has given Scotland
you will have the best possible answer to attacks
upon the Christian faith." Mr. Moody was
invited and came to Belfast. The largest churches
were crowded out from the very beginning. Mr.
Moody issued a call for prayer, in which he
said, " Again I urge, will not God's children
all over the United Kingdom meet at the noon
hour and unite their prayers with those of
Christians in different towns all over the land?
God says, ' Call upon Me, and I will answer
thee, and show thee great and mighty things
that thou knowest not.' Has not the time come
for the Church of God to arise and call upon
our God for blessing? Thousands of our
young men are fast passing to a drunkard's grave,
while numbers of our young women are going
down in the world's whirlpool. Will not the
fathers and mothers, if there is no one else
to meet, come together at the noontide hour
and ask for blessing on their children? Shall
we say there are yet four months and then
harvest, or shall we arise now and with prayer

put in the sickle and gather?" One result of the Belfast work was that two thousand professed to have passed from darkness to light, from death to life. Mr. Moody then returned to England, taking Manchester, Sheffield, Birmingham, and Liverpool on his way. Some time before this Professor Henry Drummond, of Glasgow, was led to take part in the work, and all through his help proved most valuable, especially in the inquiry meetings, and he soon became a living power in the movement. It was not long before London began to move in earnest, and it was resolved to have a special mission, extending over four months. A fund of not less than £10,000 was to be raised, and in addition to Mr. Moody and Mr. Sankey, other men with evangelistic gifts were to be invited to take part in the work. Four centres were chosen, and the meeting-places in succession were occupied with vast audiences. We were privileged to be present in the Agricultural Hall and in the Opera House. At both of these places we had also the joy of dealing with souls in the inquiry room. The blessing accompanying the preaching of the Word was very real and extensive. High and low, rich and poor, crowded to hear the Gospel, and the result was the same, a whole turning of hearts unto the Lord. Materialism and Atheism gave way before it. In Edinburgh the Secular Society was broken up. The same took place in Glasgow, and now in London it had given way before the Ark of God. Thousands who were led to yield their own selves to Christ have since then been living workers in promoting the advancement of His Kingdom.

Chapter VII

More British Campaigns

AFTER an interval of six years, Mr. Moody accepted a pressing invitation for a second mission in Great Britain and Ireland. A second time he began in Newcastle-on-Tyne, after which he devoted six weeks to Edinburgh and five months to Glasgow and neighbourhood. Men like Principal Cairns, Professor Blaikie, Dr. Andrew Bonar, Dr. Elder Cumming, Dr. Somerville, John Campbell White, Alexander Allan, John Galloway, and many others, as on the former occasion, nobly supported him. All the old features of his work were still maintained —prayer-meetings, Bible readings, evangelistic addresses—but in addition to these he gave himself specially to addressing meetings of Christian workers, and every Saturday to special services for the children. Many people would be apt to think that Mr. Moody had no gift in the latter direction. He, however, proved himself an adept in dealing with the young. During this second campaign in Glasgow the social side of Mr. Moody's work was developed with remarkable results. An organised campaign was entered on for the rescue of drunkards, and the success of the meetings in the Circus proved that the Gospel had lost none of its power to meet the most desperate cases. There are thousands in our city to-day who at that time were rescued from the power and thraldom of strong drink. During the whole time he frequently addressed two meetings each night, and sometimes three. The interest was sustained all the time, and there were literally hundreds of inquirers every night. It was on this mission that Mr. Moody was led to occupy Cowcaddens Church, and it was then that the northern district of the city received the awakening, the results of which have not died out yet. After Mr. Moody left, the work at Cowcaddens was carried on by the United Evangelistic Association, under Major A. S. D. Colquhoun and others, and in October 1883 the present writer was settled, under whose hand the work for many long years continued to prosper. After a short rest, Mr. Moody visited

Wales, from which he went to Paris for a fortnight, returning thence to England, and after a
short visit to Ireland in January, and occupying
the interval with several of the English principal
towns, he commenced a campaign in London.
Special halls were erected, Mr. Robert Paton and
Mr. Hugh M. Matheson bearing the chief part
of the burden of superintending the work. The
mission itself was most thoroughly gone into, the
whole cost being over £20,000, which was raised
by special contributions. The seating capacity
of the halls varied from five thousand upwards.
These halls were taken to the congested districts
of the city in succession. The object aimed at
was thoroughly accomplished. For once at least
the poor had the Gospel preached unto them.
These buildings were erected on eleven different
sites in succession, embracing north, south, east,
and west. Mr. Moody always spoke twice, and
sometimes four times, in a day. Altogether over
two millions of people were brought within reach
of his voice. The state of Mr. Sankey's health
necessitated his return to America before the
great mission closed. Everybody said there would
be a collapse ; but instead of that it only seemed
as if Mr. Moody were made all the more

prominent, and his work not the less blessed by the removal of his colleague. It has not been possible to make any calculation as to the results of this very singular and extended mission ; but it is not too much to say that thousands have been led to take up the cross and follow the Saviour. To Mr. Moody himself, and to his fellow-workers, there came the richest and rarest of earthly joys —the joy of a spiritual harvest.

The following may be taken as an illustration of the work accomplished in London : A gentle-man passing through America called upon Mr. Moody and said to him, " You do not know me, but I must speak to you, as I leave for California to-night, and we shall probably never meet again. Twenty-five years ago you were speaking in London, and along with two other young fellows, I wandered in to hear you. We were moral lepers, and had gone far in all kinds of sin. The Spirit of God touched our hearts that night through your words. We did not stop to speak to you, but when we came out of the hall on to the walk we shook hands and said quietly to one another, ' From this night we begin a new life.' One of the three died in Egypt at the head of his regiment, an earnest Christian soldier. The second is a heroic missionary in Africa, and I am the third." Similar testimonies might be cited a thousandfold.

The third British Campaign (1891–92) was, in some respects, the most remarkable of all. After consultation with the directors of the United Evangelistic Association in Glasgow, at the head of whom was Lord Overtoun, and amongst whom were most of the members of his former Committee, Mr. Moody resolved to devote this mission very specially to the country towns, villages, and outlying districts, practically untouched by his former visit. A memorial asking him to give that mission in Great Britain was presented at the Northfield Conference, and represented the leading Christian workers in upwards of fifty towns, cities, and villages of Scotland. It contained 2500 signatures. After consultation with several friends, and an address to ministers and other Christian workers in which Mr. John M'Neill, then of London, took a prominent part, an outlined sketch of the work proposed for himself and Mr. Sankey was made and submitted for his approval. Mr. William Ross, of Cowcaddens, was asked by the Association to go north and arrange for the work as

5

far as possible from Nairn to Caithness and back to Huntly. Mr. William Robertson, of Carrubber's Close Mission, Edinburgh, was also able to accompany Mr. Moody in the far north. All the arrangements were made, and all the engagements kept without a single hitch until he reached Aberdeen, where at New Year time, with the assistance of Mr. M'Neill, a very remarkable work was accomplished. In the centre and south of Scotland the work went on without a night's intermission until the beginning of April. The fruit of former visits in the great cities and among condensed masses of the people was very abundant, and all the churches received a great strengthening. Villages and country districts are usually much more conservative and less ready to fall in with new methods or to express their feelings with any readiness, but, if the experience on a day of snowstorm in an outlying district of Nairnshire may be taken as a sample of the work done, nothing could be more gratifying or more remarkable. The fields were not only white to the harvest, but the harvest was very abundant and very gracious. A visit to the Holy Land, through the kindness and urgency of Mr. and Mrs. Peter M'Kinnon, enabled him to realise what he himself called " a dream of his life," but one which he scarcely dared to hope would be realised on earth. Ever afterwards the memory of that visit proved one of the most fruitful topics, both in the house and public gathering, wherever Mr. Moody appeared. This third campaign in Great Britain, though occupying less space in the public press, and less prominence in the public eye, was probably the most remarkable in Mr. Moody's experience as an evangelist.

Chapter VIII

Work in America

THE work accomplished in America was enormous in extent and varied in character. It may be conveniently divided into three great departments. The first, and in some respects the most prominent of these, was the evangelistic work carried on from time to time, systematically and successfully, in great centres of population. The happiest moment in Mr. Moody's experience was when he was gathering in the wonderful harvest of a season of great power and blessing. The next happiest moment was probably when he was organising a great community towards a common centre, with a view to securing the salvation of all : to be surrounded with a body of Christian ministers and Christian workers, prayerful, sympathetic, earnest, and have one and all realise the great object of their life and work, and then to send them forth into it and permit their own eyes to see what God could accomplish by them—an hour in such work made its mark upon his heart and upon his life, while there went a thrill of joy and hope through all about him. To these great evangelistic campaigns he gave all his strength, all his energies, every concentrated thought and every intense aspiration. He could honestly say, " This one thing I do." The great cities of Canada and the United States gave him a life-work, to which, with the exception of the time he devoted to Britain, he gave himself most loyally. In them all, Mr. Sankey shared his fears and his joys, his hopes and his happiness, and contributed by his great musical faculties, as well as by his calm and controlled disposition, very largely to the success of the work. To say that hundreds of thousands during these powerful attacks upon the world and the kingdom of darkness were led to decision for Christ is to speak within the mark. Nothing less than the joy of the Lord and power from on high could sustain any man in these prolonged and arduous under-takings. Among the many cities that shared in his services, two stand out very prominent—Chicago and Boston. In the former city a special

tabernacle was erected, capable of holding ten
thousand. Ministers and Christian workers co-
operated with him in the heartiest possible manner.
The results of the missions were exceptionally
large. Mr. Moody always urged on the young
converts to strengthen themselves by union with
the Christian Church as early as possible, and
then to throw themselves right loyally into
Christian service. Before the close of his first
mission in Chicago there were thousands of
accessions to the several churches. Boston is a
very peculiar city in many ways—difficult to
attack and difficult to work. A building capable
of holding from six to seven thousand was secured.
He had the hearty co-operation of Dr. A. J.
Gordon and others. Although the work was
exceptionally hard, the results were abundantly
manifest, and the general testimony was that they
were larger than even in Edinburgh or Glasgow.
In the same way hundreds of cities were visited
and always with similar results. In Philadelphia,
to take one example, unwonted scenes occurred,
of which this description has been given :

" The Moody and Sankey meetings were
unique in the annals of Philadelphia. From the
very first day there was a tremendous pressure

for tickets, and rain or shine, for two months, weekdays and Sundays, crowds found their way to Thirteenth and Market Streets, the like of which had never before been seen in the city. The street-car lines revised their schedules and put on extra cars to take care of the traffic. Straight through the Christmas holidays the audiences kept coming. It was distinctively a laymen's movement, in which virtually all men of note participated. So thoroughly stirred was the community that the judges of the Supreme Court attended in a body, and President Grant and most of the Cabinet came from Washington to hear Moody preach and Sankey sing."

The second department in Mr. Moody's American work was what might be called " the entrance on golden opportunities." Like the angel that came down at certain seasons and troubled the waters at Bethesda, there were events that providentially occurred to awaken, arouse, and stimulate whole communities. Intellectual and physical activity were intensely roused and prolonged in connection with great public gatherings, international exhibitions, and similar movements. In ordinary church work few felt inclined to enter upon any special work on such occasions. They felt as if these were inimical to earnest spiritual service. Indeed, at such times many gave up their ordinary work, feeling that it was bound to be unsuccessful in the presence of such distracting public engagements. With Mr. Moody it was the reverse. He believed that such occasions were like a springtime, when the intellectual and moral ploughshare ought to prepare the way for spiritual sowing. Having this conviction, he recognised the value of opportunity and seldom failed to have some special service, likely to be blessed, ready for such occasions when they arose. We need only take for illustration the preparation which he had made for the World's Fair at Chicago, which he said himself was " the opportunity of a century." It is only correct to say that the work was exceptionally difficult as well as unusually large. He had less difficulty to obtain the funds than he had to secure the proper agents. In this work he had the valued assistance of Mr. John M'Neill and a large body of similar workers. In addition to tents, tabernacles, hotel parlours, and many points of interest scattered all over the city, the chief centres were Tattersall's Hall and the great circus tents. The former was capable of holding over ten thousand people, and the latter, including the standing room, could hold twice as many. Services were conducted in Polish, Hebrew, French, German, Swedish, Bohemian, and Norwegian. The leading and most powerful minds and most consecrated workers from all parts of the world were concentrated upon these. Two hours of a midday service and evening gatherings were the ordinary staple food supplied for the spiritual wants of the millions that gathered at the World's Fair. At an expenditure of £12,000 this special mission was carried on to a successful issue. In the words of Dr. Frederick Campbell, it may be said, that Mr. Moody " once more proved himself to be a most remarkable instrument in the hands of providence for working out Divine plans."

Of this great World's Fair Campaign one writes : " It is impossible to tabulate the good results of the work undertaken and effected. Figures and records fail utterly to embrace the whole fact. Suffice it to say, that multitudes of all classes and conditions of the unconverted, as well as professed Christians, were savingly affected by the Gospel as it was preached and sung. Conversions were of daily occurrence, sometimes numbering scores in a single meeting, especially in the services held in theatres and tents. Here some of the lowest and vilest of city slum-dwellers were gloriously saved; many a wild, reckless visitor from afar was brought home to God. In addition, many thousands of Christian men and women were renewed, instructed, strengthened, and inspired for better life and service."

The third department of his American work may be denominated " Bible Training for Christian Workers." It seems strange to say so, and yet there is some truth in the statement that there are Christian workers more familiar with books, addresses, material, and men connected with Christian labour than they are with the Bible itself, which is the great text-book on salvation and service. In his movements throughout America and the British Islands it was deeply impressed upon the mind of Mr. Moody that there was a great lack of persons capable and eager for dealing with inquirers, or for handling effectively public gatherings for Christian work. Between the college-trained man and the humble Sunday-school teacher or visitor there is a great gap which ought to be filled by a body of trained men and women, and the question came to be with him how this gap was to be worthily filled. The idea of the Bible Training Institute occurred to him, where courses of lectures on the Scriptures and on methods of Christian work could be delivered with advantage by intellectually strong and spiritually powerful Christian men. To see the need for such an institution was with Mr. Moody all that was required. It must be started at once. There was no time for delay, and there was no necessity. The work must be done, and so the Bible Training Institute in Chicago and the Scholastic Institute at Mount Hermon and North-field took their rise, and have been carried on with increasing success until this very day. At the close of his last evangelistic campaign in Scotland, the writer of these lines was sitting on the platform of the noonday meeting. When the benediction was pronounced, and the large audience was separating, Mr. Moody put his hand upon his shoulder and said, " You are going to New Zealand ? " He replied, " That is my intention." " When are you going ? " " All being well, on the 25th of August." " Then you must go by Chicago and lecture at the Bible Training Institute for ten days, and tell them how to win souls for

Christ, and tell them of the blessing which God has given you at Cowcaddens." He replied, " It is not possible. It is not for me. I am going away to rest." He simply called the Secretary, and without another word, said, " Wire to the Bible Training Institute, Chicago, that Mr. Ross will be there early in September to give a course of lectures on ' How to Win Souls for Christ.' " There was no opportunity for refusal or denial. The work must be done. It has to be said that never in any work had the writer greater joy or larger blessing than in connection with this opportunity. He had also the privilege of seeing all the departments of service, and of knowing that, notwithstanding the great expense of carrying on such institutions, Mr. Moody was admirably supported by a large body of generous givers and prayerful servants of Christ, whose joy it was to spend and be spent for Him. In this work he has not only done what he could, but has left behind him a legacy to the Church and Christian agencies throughout the world that will increasingly be a power and a blessing in the ages to come.

Chapter IX

A New Experience

FOR several years there had been in the minds of several evangelistic workers in Scotland the thought that there was room and a call for an institute on similar lines to that which Mr. Moody had so successfully established at Chicago. Some correspondence took place in regard to it with leading men, a plan of operations embracing the three principal cities was sketched, but the matter never came to any issue until the annual meeting of the United Evangelistic Association in Glasgow, when Mr. Moody, in his own candid way, on the platform in St. Andrew's Hall, started and developed the whole scheme, and then asked several of the leading directors, including Lord Overtoun, the Chairman, Mr. Jas. S. Napier, Mr. Galloway, and others, whether they would support such a movement, and receiving an answer in the affirmative, it was resolved at once to start the Bible Training Institute, which now forms part of the handsome block of buildings which grace Bothwell Street on the north side. Steps were at once taken to organise the institute, one of the first necessities being to find a man of God, intellectually strong, apt to teach, easy to co-operate with, firm in action, and capable of commanding respect as the head of such an institution. This was readily found in the person of Mr. John Anderson, of Ardrossan, who carried on the work with singular aptitude and success from its beginning for twenty-one years. Till a suitable building in which the institute could be housed was procured, it was necessary to occupy premises elsewhere, and 1 Blythswood Square proved to be the first home of the Bible Training Institute. Students came from all quarters, and the place was filled. The first year's work was amply sufficient to prove the wisdom of the step that had been taken, and the work that was capable of being accomplished in the interests of the Kingdom of Christ, and that, too, without interference with any university or college

in the country. An additional year's experience
only demonstrated the necessity of obtaining
a larger building, and through the generous
consideration of the late Mrs. J. E. Somerville,
and the President of the Evangelistic Association, Lord Overtoun, a site was procured, and
the present extensive buildings, to which they
so generously contributed, reared in a position
which is second to none in Glasgow. At first
the directors only contemplated receiving male
students ; indeed, they had accommodation for
no others. By and by the pressure became so
great from ladies applying to have the privilege
of training, that the directors had to yield and
arrange for their accommodation outside, while
they enjoyed the common training in Blythswood Square and the Christian Institute, where
the classes had latterly to be held. The opening
of the Institute was a great day in Glasgow.
Lord Overtoun presided, and was assisted by
the leading men of the city, who took a deep
interest in the new movement. The experience
which each year as it passes furnishes, only
shows that for home and foreign mission work,
it has secured a class of agent, which is so thoroughly in demand, that not a single student of

former years is now out of employment. Large
numbers have gone to the foreign field; many
are employed at home, and a few have gone
to college, pursuing their studies with a view to
the ministry of the Gospel for one or other of
the Evangelical Churches. The staff has had
to be enlarged in accordance with the growing
capacity and extension of the Institute. At the
same time, the work became more thoroughly
consolidated, and the labours of Mr. Anderson
and his assistants more abundantly owned of
God.

Mr. Moody had a strange yearning for extending his evangelistic labours to parts of the
world hitherto unvisited. India and China lay
heavy on his heart. It was a great disappoint-
ment to him, therefore, when he learned, after
examination by two of the first physicians in
Britain, that it would not be wise for him to
face the climate of these eastern lands, especially
at his time of life, and with a susceptibility to
heat exhaustion.

After leaving Scotland he devoted some time
to Ireland and to England, and very gracious
results followed his mission to these parts.

On the voyage home from Southampton to

New York he passed through an experience which left its mark upon him for the remainder of his life. Through the breaking of a shaft the steamer was in great danger, and at one time supposed to be sinking. Passengers rushed on deck, and for two days the ship drifted in a helpless condition, every effort being made, however, to save her. Captain, officers, and crew did their very utmost to save both the vessel and the precious lives on board. Mr. Moody himself describes the condition of things : " There was nothing more in the power of man to do, and the ship was absolutely helpless, while the passengers could only stand there on the poor drifting, sinking vessel, and look into their possible watery graves. Life-boats were all put in readiness, provisions were prepared, life-preservers were brought out. the officers were armed with revolvers so as to be able to enforce their orders, and it was only a question of whether to launch the boats at once or wait. The sea was so heavy that the boats could hardly live in it." Their only hope was that they might drift in the way of a ship during the day or afternoon, but the darkness of night came without the sight of a single sail. Mr. Moody says : " That was an awful night—

6

the darkest in all our lives. Several hundred
men, women, and children, waiting for the doom
that seemed to be settling upon us. The agony
and suspense were too great for words. Rockets
flamed into the sky, but there was no answer.
We were drifting out of the track of the great
steamers. Every hour seemed to increase the
danger." Sunday morning appeared. Until
then no one proposed to have any religious
service. On the second night, however, Mr.
Moody secured the Captain's consent, and nearly
every passenger on board attended. Mr. Moody
read the 91st Psalm, and prayed that God might
still the raging of the sea, and bring them to their
desired haven. He says himself : " It was a
new Psalm for me from that hour. The eleventh
verse touched me very deeply. It was like a
voice of Divine assurance, and it seemed a very
real thing as I read, ' He shall give His angels
charge over thee, to keep thee in all thy ways.'
I read from Psalm cvii. 20 to 31. One lady
actually thought these words must have been
written for the occasion, and afterwards asked
to see the Book for herself. A German trans-
lated for the benefit of his countrymen." I was
passing," he says, " through a new experience.

I had thought myself superior to the fear of
death. I had often preached on the subject.
In the Civil War I had been under fire without
fear. I was in Chicago during the great cholera
epidemic. I remember a case of small-pox
where the sufferer's condition was beyond description. Yet I went to the bedside of that poor
sufferer, again and again, with Bible and prayer
for Jesus' sake. In all this I had no fear of death ;
but on the sinking ship it was different. There
was no cloud between my soul and my Saviour,
but as my thoughts went out to my beloved
ones at home, my wife, my children, my friends
on both sides of the sea, the school and all the
interests so dear to me, and as I realised that
perhaps the next hour would part me for ever
from all these so far as this world was concerned,
it almost broke me down. It was the darkest
hour of my life. I found relief in prayer. God
heard my cry and enabled me to say from the
depth of my soul, ' Thy will be done.' Sweet
peace came to my heart." About three o'clock
in the morning a far-off light was seen. It proved
to be the light of a passing steamer. " Oh !
the joy of that moment, when the seven hundred
despairing passengers beheld the approaching

ship. Who can ever forget it?" They were towed back to Queenstown, and taking a passage on the *Etruria*, now cured of sea-sickness, he enjoyed the voyage home, to which he received a right royal welcome.

CHAPTER X

The Man and his Methods

AS these pages are intended to be helpful to Christian workers, one naturally expects to find some points in such a life as Mr. Moody's that might prove suggestive and be of value in practical service. The foregoing pages show that Mr. Moody's life was exceptionally *busy*, " Seest thou a man diligent in his business, he shall stand before kings, he shall not stand before mean men." But although so busy, he was in a great part of his life (his family circle always excepted) individual and solitary. Deep in his soul his thoughts and purposes and plans were formed. In private prayer, meditation, and reflection, all his treasures were found, and the wealth and the worth of them appeared in public. Like the mountain - stream that gathers strength as it descends from the heights, so the force of character and action acquired strength in his fellowship with God. But he was a man of great *capacity*. He was influenced on many sides by many men and many things. Those that were kin to his work, clung to him as steel filings to a magnet. He had the wonderful power also of influencing men of diverse pursuits and dispositions in one direction. His power of *concentration* was equally remarkable. Asleep, awake, resting, working, praying, talking, studying or speaking, his mind had but one bias, one direction, and was centred on one point, " How to glorify Christ in the salvation of men." Few men since the days of Paul could say with greater truth, " This one thing I do." " I love the Lord Jesus Christ, and I want to do something for Him," were the words with which he began his earliest efforts, and they characterised that work to the end. From this habit of mind naturally there sprung his *thoroughness*. He could do nothing by halves, neither could he tolerate other people doing so. In the very details of the work, issuing tickets, visiting, circulars, bills, everything must be thorough. So in the public service, singing, reading, prayer, as well as speaking, everything must be animated, pointed, informing, subduing. In choosing a subject he would consider whether he would have a single service, a few meetings, or a prolonged series ; if the first, he invariably selected one that was full of the *love of God in Christ Jesus*. A discourse or address was for him a weapon which he must wield with freedom and with a purpose. He must make the most of it. All these qualifications would be of comparatively little avail without his large and definite *sympathy* and *compassion* for the perishing. He truthfully said, " I know what it is to pray over men's souls and to weep over men's sins." He identified himself with those whom he addressed ; but in all the work he sought nothing for himself. He only desired liberty and opportunity to serve Christ. Herein lay the *secret of his great strength*, in that he was filled and fitted by the Spirit of Christ. He was thus usable and used to glorify the Master whom he served.

In method he was not only a master, but he was constantly *growing*, and with a fuller knowledge and experience acquiring fresh aptitude. Some Christian workers are naturally limited in range of thought, in vocabulary, and expression. They are stereotyped in method, and fail in adapting themselves to new circumstances or to

an increasing light. They are apt to be critical,
fault-finding, censorious, if not cruel in regard
to all methods except their own, and to all workers
who differ from them. It was very different
with Mr. Moody, he was catholic and kindly.
The young man of twenty-two, like Henry
Drummond, and the old, like Dr. Bonar and
Dr. Cairns, were equally esteemed, beloved, and
welcomed. His library largely consisted of his
Bible and the record of its glorious victories.
His experimental acquaintance with it kept him
always full and fresh. He was original, catholic,
and consistent. He was always open to suggestion
and improvement. When he began, he had a
strong impression that evangelisation lay specially
within the sphere of the Young Men's Christian
associations, as furnishing a large and a catholic
basis, and he did his best on these lines, and it
was a fruitful best. This idea held him probably
till 1874 or 1875.

A few more years' experience of such work as
the Lord sent him, led him to see that while it
was good to work in halls, or such places as
people could be gathered in, there was always a
large percentage of loss in more than one direction. He then came to see that it could be done

with better husbandry of results *in* churches, if only they would unite. During the last few years of his life, while not neglecting such openings for service, and such agencies as he had known to be blessed, he was convinced that for permanent, masterful, far-reaching service, it must be done *by* living churches, which should carefully husband the results. He had practically fallen on the lines of Dr. Chalmers's territorial system. Three years before his death he caused Dr. Gray, of Boston, to communicate with the writer of these lines, asking him to furnish materials connected with the history of the movement in Cowcaddens—its progress and results —in the hope that Dr. Gray might be able to publish a little volume that might give the Churches confidence and comfort in *aiming at completely overtaking the clamant necessities of the great cities* of America and of the world. But Mr. Moody was no sectarian. He said, " God had vouchsafed to Christians a blessed unity, woe to the unhappy person who should break it." His own great aim was to unite all Christians in great, prayerful, resolute effort to win souls for Christ.

Moreover, in all his service he was wholeheartedly yielded to God.

One of his addresses began with the striking phrase—" Since I left the world forty years ago." One who heard him say this remarked afterwards : " Yes, that is the reason Moody has done so much for the world. Because he left it forty years ago, the whole world has been much benefited by him. Is not that the reason so few Christians seem to win ? Is it not because they have not left the world ? What is it to leave the world ? There was a world of men and women which Mr. Moody did not leave until his death, for thousands of earnest truth-seekers crowded to hear him until a few weeks before he passed away. While he lived he loved the world of Nature, for at Northfield no one enjoyed more keenly the sunshine of a summer day or the glittering white robe of snow which covered the land in winter. Then, what world did he leave forty years before ? I went back in memory to thirty years before when Mr. Moody came to Bridgeport, where I then lived. The bell of the old Presbyterian Church rang out at nine o'clock on Sunday morning, but Mr. Moody had not depended on the bell. He had gone from store to store through the streets of Bridgeport on the Saturday evening on his arrival, and he had persuaded his relative with whom he was staying to take the other side of the street, and invite the people to come out at nine o'clock the next morning. And they came, for the personal appeal was irresistible. How well I remember that Sunday! The good that was then accomplished was the result of Moody's having ' left the world.' He left the world that he might win it."

Chapter XI

The Valley of the Shadow

MR. MOODY'S service for Christ in public
was *work*. His *rest* was in the bosom of
his family. He counted it a privilege and
an honour to be used of God in his world-wide
mission, but his greatest joy and peace and
growth were in the family circle. His four
months at home were as fruitful as those spent
in the public eye. He said it nearly broke his
heart when he heard his sister tell that in early
life his mother wept herself to sleep every night.
Her children woke up and heard her praying.
This shows that he was a man of strong affections.
To wife and children, as well as to his mother,
he was devoted. He said they were his greatest
earthly helps.

In November 1899 he was pursuing a fruitful
mission in Kansas City in the large Convention
Hall. For some days he seemed to enjoy the

work as heartily as heretofore. The crowds were larger, the singing heartier and fresher, and the results were wonderful. But the breakdown even of his strong constitution was at hand. On 12th November he wrote Mrs. Mackinnon: " The work is sweeter now than ever, and I think I have some streams started that will flow on for ever. What a joy to be in the harvest-field and have a hand in God's work."

Near the close of one of the services he remarked: " Will you ministers allow me to say a word to you ? " " Yes, yes ; say what you want," they replied. " Well, I'm not a prophet, but I have a guess to make that I think will prove a true prophecy. You hear so much nowadays about the preacher of the twentieth century. Do you know what sort of a man he will be ? He will be the sort of preacher who opens his Bible and preaches out of that. Oh ! I'm sick tired of this essay preaching ! I'm nauseated with this silver-tongued orator preaching. I like to hear preachers and not windmills."

A telegram to his family was the first intimation of his illness. A heart trouble had manifested itself in an aggravated form. It was practically his first and last illness.

His son, Mr. W. R. Moody, whose full and beautiful " Life " of his father has laid the Christian world under obligations, tells us no man loved his family and life-work more devotedly, and he had often said : " Life is very sweet to me, and there is no position of power or wealth that could tempt me from the throne God has given me." His illness continued with such intervals of relief as gave hope for recovery, but on 22nd December 1899 the shadow of death was turned into the morning. About six o'clock he was saying : " Earth recedes, Heaven opens before me. It is beautiful ; it is like a trance ; if this is death, it is sweet ; there is no valley here ; God is calling me, and I must go ; this is my triumph ; this is my coronation day. I have been looking forward to it for years."

Long ago he said : " I was born of the flesh in 1837 ; I was born of the Spirit in 1856. That which is born of the flesh may die ; that which is born of the Spirit will live for ever."

Dr. Campbell Morgan, who had preached at Northfie d in the previous autumn, gives the following description of how the news of the great evangelist's death reached him :

" It was on Saturday morning last. I had

taken my seat in a train at Birmingham Station to return to London. My journey to Birmingham had been taken for the transaction of business on behalf of Dwight L. Moody at his special request. Though the morning was black with fog I was in excellent spirits, for I was returning to communicate to him by the very next mail the probable success of my mission. I took up my newspaper and was reading the account of the death of the Duke of Westminster. My eye wandered, and then my heart nearly stood still, for the very next column was headed, ' Death of Mr. Moody.' The account was brief. He had died at his residence of ' failure of the heart.' That was the blunt, brutal newspaper account. I do not blame the Press. What more could they say ? We knew that in all the higher and truer senses of the word he was not dead, nor had his heart failed. He had passed to the truer life, and his great heart had commenced to move in absolute accord with the rhythm of the divine."

His remains were laid to rest on Round Top on 26th December. A large concourse of loving and devoted friends accompanied the loved ones of the family to the grave. The keynote of all the service was the keynote of his own life, and the secret of comfort in his death. " Thanks be unto God, who giveth us the victory through our Lord Jesus Christ."

Professor Drummond, writing to a friend on 20th December 1882, said : " My admiration for Mr. Moody has increased a hundredfold. I had no idea before of the moral size of the man, and I think very few know what he really is." A month before his death Mr. Drummond said to one of the doctors : " Moody was the biggest human I ever met."

After thus running rapidly through a life beautified and blessed by the grace of God, and of one who served his generation according to the will of God, we may well ask that our Covenant God may make us " followers of them who through faith and patience do now inherit the promises," and that the same grace may enable us to live so that at the end we may hear the voice : " Well done, good and faithful servant, enter thou into the joy of thy Lord."